Contents

Words printed in **bold** are explained in the glossary

What are clothes like?

How would you manage without clothes? They keep you warm in cold weather and dry in the wet. They protect your skin from the wind and hot sun and keep you snug at night.

Cotton clothes are fine and smooth. Cotton lets your skin breathe. It soaks up sweat and keeps you cool in hot weather.

T-shirts are made of knitted cotton.

Jeans are made of a tough kind of cotton **fabric** called denim.

Woollen clothes are soft and springy.

Wool traps air between its **fibres** and keeps you warm in cold weather.

re-using & recycling

Clothes

Ruth Thomson

Photography by Neil Thomson

FRANKLIN WATTS
LONDON • SYDNEY

First published in 2006 by
Franklin Watts
338 Euston Road
London NW1 3BH

Franklin Watts Australia
Hachette Children's Books
Level 17/207 Kent Street
Sydney NSW 2000

Text copyright © Ruth Thomson 2006
Photographs copyright © Neil Thomson 2006

Editor: Rachel Cooke
Design: Holly Mann
Art Director: Rachel Hamdi
Consultant: Michelle Barry, LMB London

Additional photography
Thanks are due to the following for kind
permission to reproduce photographs:
Franklin Watts 6, 7, 11b, 15b, 21tr; Picanol 9c,
LMB London 10r, 12; Recycle now 10bl, 11t,
26t; Lucy Bateman and Etienne Oliff 27tr
and c; Jenny Matthews 12 and 26br

ISBN 0 7496 6102 X

A CIP catalogue record for this book is
available from the British Library.

Dewey Decimal Classification Number: 687

Printed in China

Acknowledgements
The author and publisher wish to thank the
following people for their help with this book:
Adri Schutz and Zanele Sinuka at *Miele*;
Madebeza Siziba, Noxolile Ngoyiyana and
Nomonde Noludwe at the *Philani Project*,
Cape Town, South Africa; Maria Aparecida,
Yole Milani Medeiros and Cintia Cimbaluk in
Curitiba, Brazil; Leila Iskandar at *APE*, Cairo,
Egypt; Mohammed Sameh Mohammed,
Ahmed Hegazy and Osama Ali; Justine Skeels
and Ellen Baker at *Junky Styling*, London;
Elspeth Murray, Sue Adler, Vanessa Applebaum
and Mark Watson.

Some clothes are made of **synthetic** fabrics. These are usually very strong.

Some synthetic fabrics are waterproof.

Some synthetic fabrics are stretchy.

Look at the labels on your clothes to find out what they are made from.

Clothes are washable.
When clothes get dirty, they can be washed in soap and water to make them clean again.

Rip!
If you catch your clothes on something sharp, they will tear.

Making textiles

Textiles for clothes are made from long, thin, bendy threads, known as fibres.

Fine fibres

Natural fibres come from animals, plants or insects. Synthetic fibres are made in factories from oil, coal and wood.

Acrylic fibres are made from oil.

Woollen fibres come from the coats of sheep, goats or rabbits.

Cotton fibres come from the seed-head of the cotton plant.

Silk fibres come from the cocoons that silkworms spin.

Wool from a sheep is dirty and greasy.

Cleaned wool is spun and **dyed**.

Spinning

The fibres must be stretched and twisted so that they overlap to make long threads, called **yarn**. This is called spinning.

Reels of spun cotton thread

Weaving

Most yarn is woven on a **loom**. A loom holds taut lengthwise threads, spaced closely side by side. These are called the warp yarns. Another thread, called the weft yarn, criss-crosses the warp yarns, from one side to the other.

Warp yarns

Weft yarn

Factory looms

Huge automatic looms weave cloth in **factories**. Blasts of air or metal arms move the weft yarn to and fro.

Knitting

Yarn can also be knitted. Knitting uses one long yarn which is looped and knotted together in rows.

LOOK AND SEE

Try stretching a pair of jeans and a knitted scarf. The scarf is stretchier. The knitted loops become wider as you pull. Denim jeans are tightly woven. The threads cannot stretch very far.

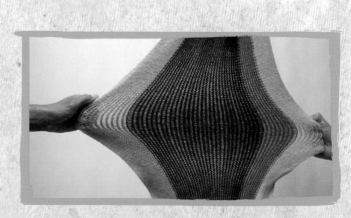

Giving away clothes

It is a waste to throw away clothes that you have out-grown or no longer want.

Filling up landfill
If you put clothes with your rubbish, they will just be buried at a **landfill site** and take up valuable space.

Clothing banks
Put clean, unwanted clothes into a clothing bank. You could also give them to a charity shop.

Sorted by hand
The clothes go to a huge warehouse. Here, skilled people carefully sort them by type, size and material.

Charity shops

When people buy second-hand clothes in charity shops, they help raise money for that charity.

YOU CAN HELP

- *Pass on clothes that no longer fit to smaller friends, brothers or sisters.*
- *Put unwanted clothes in plastic bags to keep them clean and dry for taking to a clothing bank.*
- *Cut up old cotton clothes to use as cleaning rags.*
- *Use old clothes for messy activities.*

Re-used or recycled

Good clothes can be worn again.
Unwearable clothes are cut or shredded.

Second-hand sales

Many second-hand clothes are resold to Africa, Asia and
Eastern Europe. Shops and market traders sell
the clothes cheaply to people who could
not afford more expensive new clothes.

Nothing wasted

Very worn T-shirts, sweatshirts and cotton
trousers are cut up and turned into
wiping cloths for all types of cleaning.

Buttons and zips are cut off
clothes used as wiping cloths.

Shredded into 'shoddy'

Completely unusable clothes are **recycled**. They are torn into fibres which are known as **shoddy**. To make shoddy, these **waste pickers** in Egypt feed clothes by hand into a machine.

Shoddy

The clothes go in one end. . .

. . . and come out the other end as shoddy.

Padding and filling

This delivery man in Morocco is bringing shoddy to a furniture workshop. It will be used as mattress filling or chair and sofa padding. Shoddy is also used as sound **insulation** material.

Crafty clothes

Some fashion designers create new garments combining pieces of second-hand clothes.

A wacky waistcoat

The waistcoat below is made from several printed silk scarves. They were sewn together and cut into shape.

A shirt skirt

Can you see the sleeves of an old shirt which make up part of this skirt?

Detail of the waistcoat pockets

An unusual belt

This belt is made with men's ties. The cut ends have been sewn onto the waistband of an old pair of jeans.

Hand-crafted hats

Some designers recycle unusual materials into new hats.

A hat made from the front of a woolly cardigan

Tough tarpaulin

Some Brazilian designers make caps and hats, as well as bags and jackets, from old **tarpaulin**.

A summer hat woven from rolled paper

A cowboy hat made from pieces of old jeans

A tarpaulin cap

15

Cutting up clothes

People also cut up old clothes and use the pieces to make something completely different.

A patterned prayer rug

A rugmaker used cloth **snippets** for this tufty rug. Notice how she carefully arranged the snippets by colour to make patterns.

A stripy mat

This floor mat was woven with long strips cut from old clothes.

A smart saddle seat

Clothes scraps were poked through a piece of **hessian** to make the saddle seat on this donkey.

A patchwork folder

The cover of this folder is made from scraps of fabric sewn together.

A sock puppet

Don't throw away odd or worn socks. Make funny puppets with them.

Sew on buttons for the eyes, nose and mouth.

A pretty photo album

Sparkly cloth scraps decorate the front of this photo album.

Waste not, want not

When factories cut out clothes, there is always fabric left over. The pieces are known as **offcuts**.

Offcut originals

Girls at a school for waste pickers in Cairo learn how to weave rugs and bags with offcuts.

1. They learn to sort the offcuts by colour and material.

2. This girl is weaving offcuts on a loom. She leaves the ends loose.

3. She takes the finished fabric off the loom and trims it. Then she sews up the sides to make a bag.

The handles are made of plaited offcuts.

Patchwork pieces

Egyptian craftswomen make **patchworks** with offcuts. They cut out pieces of fabric that will fit together, using card shapes as a guide. These shapes are called templates.

Card template

Comfy cushions

They sew the pieces together to make cushion covers.

Saving scraps

In countries where cloth is expensive, people save every spare scrap.

Teeny bikinis

This dressmaker in Brazil uses tiny pieces of cloth left over from making tops to make bikinis.

Stylish scrunchies

Some people make hair scrunchies like these, by threading elastic through fabric scraps.

Rag dolls

People often make rag dolls for children from cloth scraps.

English rag dolls

Dolls from Burkina Faso

A doll from Mozambique

A clown from India

Trick cyclists

Kenyan children make toy bikes and riders by bending scrap wire. They stuff and dress the bikers with fabric scraps.

T-shirt strips

When factories make T-shirt fabric, there are long strips left over. Craftspeople use these to make all sorts of things.

Balls of T-shirt fabric strips

A woven wall hanging

1. This weaver has tied lengths of string from top to bottom of a wooden frame. She weaves the fabric strips between the strings.

2. She weaves different colours in turn to build up a picture.

3. She pushes down the strips into place with a toothed tool.

Each weaver chooses a different picture or pattern to make.

Brand-new bags

The fabric strips are also used to make handbags.

1. The maker prods the strips through a shaped piece of hessian.

2. She builds up a pattern, which covers the hessian.

3. She sews up the sides of the hessian and adds a zip to finish the bag.

Finished bags on sale

Cotton paper

In India, people recycle cuttings from white cotton T-shirts and work gloves into handmade paper (right).

Paper with strands of **algae**

Paper with sugar cane fibres

Paper with wool fibres

Paper with marigold petals

Paper with recycled **jute** sacks

Making paper

The cotton is shredded into tiny pieces, soaked and beaten into **pulp** by a machine. Sometimes dye is added to colour the paper.

1. The pulp is poured onto a **mould and deckle**, which sit in a vat of water.

3. The paper is tipped onto a piece of **felt**. This soaks up some more of the water.

2. When they are lifted out, water drains away, leaving a sheet of very wet paper on the **mesh** of the mould.

4. The paper is stacked with other sheets in a press, which squeezes out more water. Finally the sheets are separated and hung up to dry.

Patterned paper

Cotton paper is made into sketch books, photo frames, notebooks and photograph albums.

Paper bags

Photo frames

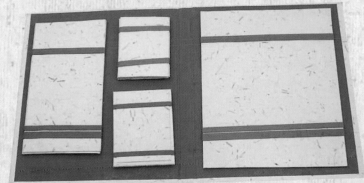

Writing set

Notebooks

Writing paper and envelopes speckled with old bank-notes

Saving shoes

Do you throw away your unwanted or outgrown shoes when you buy new ones? Most discarded shoes are re-usable.

Resoled and resold

Put unwanted shoes and sandals into a shoe or clothing bank. Some pairs of shoes are sold in charity shops. Many more are sent to countries where new shoes are expensive.

Cobblers make the shoes as good as new. Market traders resell them at prices local people can afford.

Flip-flop-a-lu-la

Hundreds of old flip-flops wash on to the beach of a marine nature reserve in Kenya. Local women collect them along with their firewood. This helps keep the beach clean and the women also make money by turning the flip-flops into toys and jewellery.

They cut up the flip-flops, shaping them into bath toys and key rings.

Flip-flop key rings

Jazzy jewellery

Some of the women string small pieces of flip-flops together into bracelets and necklaces. They add shells as extra decoration.

Bracelet

Necklace

Glossary

algae a type of plant, such as seaweed

dyed given a new colour

fabric cloth

factory a building where things are made in large numbers using machines

felt a sheet of thick matted wool

fibre a thin strand that comes from a plant or an animal, or is made artificially from oil, coal or wood pulp

hessian a strong fabric made from the jute plant

insulation a covering that stops something, such as heat, electricity or sound, passing through it

jute a tall plant with strong stringy fibres used for bags, ropes and sacks

landfill site a huge pit in the ground where crushed rubbish is buried

loom equipment for weaving fabric

mesh criss-crossed wires with tiny holes between them

mould and deckle handmade paper-making equipment. The mould is a frame with wire mesh stretched over it. The deckle is a frame with edges that hold the pulp in place

offcuts the small pieces of cloth left once a pattern has been cut out

patchwork small pieces of fabric sewn together in a pattern or picture

pulp a mass of soft, broken down fibres mixed with water for paper-making

recycle to use an existing object or material to make something new

shoddy the torn-up fibres of old clothes

snippet a little piece of fabric cut with scissors

synthetic made by people or machines not by nature

tarpaulin tough, waterproof material spread over goods in a open truck or boat to protect them from getting wet

textile a woven or knitted fabric

waste picker someone who makes a living collecting and sorting rubbish

waterproof not letting water in or out

yarn spun thread

Guess what?

- Clothes and other textiles, such as sheets, curtains and blankets, make up between 3 and 5 per cent of household rubbish.

- More than 70 per cent of the world uses second-hand clothes. Almost any clothes you don't want anymore – including swimwear, trainers, football strips, caps, ski suits, nightwear and even socks – will be useful to someone somewhere.

- Synthetic clothes do not rot in landfill sites, so it is better to pass them on than to throw them away.

- In the West, most clothes are thrown away because they have gone out of fashion, not because they are worn-out, outgrown or torn.

Useful websites

ollierecycles.com
A fun, interactive site for children about about recycling, including a section about textiles.

e4s.org.uk/textilesonline/world.htm
Information and games about textiles and recycling.

www.wasteonline.org.uk
Downloadable fact sheets about recycling, including textiles.

Some charities that collect clothes for re-using or recycling

· Oxfam
www.oxfam.org

· TRAID (Textile Recycling for Aid and Development)
www.traid.org.uk

· Scope
www.scope.org.uk/recycling

Recycling trainers
www.nikereuseashoe.com

Index